FRAGRANT FLOWERS

A GARDEN STYLE BOOK

[SIMPLE SECRETS FOR GLORIOUS GARDENS—INDOORS AND OUT]

GEORGEANNE BRENNAN

PHOTOGRAPHY BY FAITH ECHTERMEYER

CHRONICLE BOOKS

SAN FRANCISCO

Dedicated to Jim with love.–G.B.

To Bruce with love.–F.E.

Library of Congress Cataloging-in-Publication Data
Brennan, Georgeanne, 1943-
Fragrant flowers: simple secrets for glorious
gardens—indoors and out / by Georgeanne Brennan;
photography by Faith Echtermeyer.

    p.   cm.
"A Garden Style Book."
Includes index.
ISBN 0-8118-0553-0
1. Fragrant gardens. 2. Aromatic plants.
3. Flowers. I. Title.
SB454.3.F7B73 1994
635.968–dc20   93-8863
                              CIP

Printed in Hong Kong

Cover and interior design by
Aufuldish & Warinner

Distributed in Canada by Raincoast Books,
112 East Third Ave., Vancouver, B.C. V5T 1C8

10 9 8 7 6 5 4 3 2 1

Chronicle Books
275 Fifth Street
San Francisco, CA 94103

Contents

Growing fragrant flowers adds a powerful dimension to the pleasures of gardening. One whiff of a remembered smell brings a recollection of another time, another place, other feelings, and words spoken and unspoken. For me, burying my face in sweet peas freshly cut from my garden, my nostrils filling with the flowers' clean spicy fragrance immediately evokes Maytime in my grandmother's backyard, when the old wire fence was a wall of the blooms in purple, rose, red, and pastels. I can hear clearly her voice as I pick the flowers. Every line on her face is plainly visible, as is the sturdy bombazine of the black dress with its small white print. As she hugs me to her, the edges of her starched homemade apron scratch my face, and I can still feel myself wiggling away. The memory elicited by the sweet peas has a discrete life, and the power of the scent takes me from my grandmother's yard on to her kitchen and in through my feelings like a film unfolding, reel after reel.

¶Flowers cut and brought into the warmth of the house, or grown in a sunny window box or on an indoor table, exhibit an intensity of fragrance that, were they outside, could be dissipated or, in cool temperatures, go unremarked. When I leave a bouquet of lilacs, lilies, and roses in the closed house for several hours, by my return they have created a veritable logjam of mingled scents.

¶Growing fragrant flowers, in spite of the glamour associated with them, is not difficult. Many fragrant flowers are quite easy to grow from seeds, indoors or out, such as sweet peas, garden pinks, and datura. Grown from bulbs, narcissus, hyacinths, freesias, and some tulips have tremendous fragrance and readily grow inside or outside, each possessing all the nutrients needed to develop and flower. The gardener provides sunlight, water, and soil.

¶For the pleasure and the fragrance of flowering trees, shrubs, and vines it is often simplest to purchase a plant already a year or two old, since, although they can be grown from seed, the plants may not flower for years or they may not grow true to type. Rosemary, citrus, and sweet daphne are among those that can be successfully grown inside, while lilac, jasmine, wisteria, and some roses perform best outdoors.

¶Our world abounds in wonderfully fragrant flowers and plants, and it was difficult to choose those few that fill this book. Since smell and the perception of fragrance are intensely personal, all of the flowers included are ones that are personal favorites of mine. I have omitted, for example, bearded iris, whose musky scent rebuffs me but which is the favorite fragrance of one of my good friends. To her its odor is the sweet, fresh, water smell of Minnesota that permeates the memories of her own early years.

Plants that produce strongly scented flowers do not belong to any one botanical category. Rather they occur throughout the range of genera and species, and there is as much botanical difference between hyacinths and datura, for example, as there is between corn and pears. Yet within this vastness of the differences, they share the common quality of having strongly scented flowers.

¶The botanical purpose of scent in flowers is primarily sexual. Scent, whether fragrant and thus pleasing to the human nose or acrid and off-putting, has evolved in the flowers as an attractant to pollinators, generally insects. The scent is produced in glands located in the petals, and there the insects find the advertised food—nectar or pollen. In the process of rummaging for the food the insects brush against the pollen-laden anthers, coating themselves, and then, in the same flower or another one, brush against the female stigma, effecting pollination.

¶Some plants have aromatic leaves and stems rather than flower parts, so pollination is not the only rationale for the evolutionary change. Why the producing glands occur in plant parts other than the flower is not currently understood, but one school of thought gives the oils that scent the leaves, often slightly bitter to the taste, a role in the deterrence of predatory insects.

¶It is acknowledged that many of the most fragrant flowers are those that are white or pastels. Lacking brilliance of color to attract pollinators for fertilization, they rely on scent.

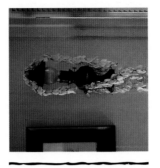

¶Scented flowers may be annuals, perennials, or biennials. Annuals are plants that complete their life cycle within a year's time. They germinate, grow, bloom, fertilize, produce seeds, and die within twelve months. Sweet peas, heliotrope, stock, and some datura are examples.

¶Perennials are plants that live more than two years, and many live considerably longer. These include both trees and shrubs, as well as bulbs, but generally the term perennials is used in reference to herbaceous, less woody plants. Some perennials lose their leaves and become dormant, as do lilac, roses, and wisteria. Others, such as violets, die back in winter. Still others, such as rosemary, sweet daphne, and kumquat trees, are evergreen.

¶Biennials live only two years and take that long to complete their life cycle, growing the first year and reproducing the second. Short-lived perennials are often grouped with the biennials.

¶Annual flowers are generally quick to grow and to bloom. They rarely fail to perform well in full sun in nearly any garden soil or potting mix, providing they have adequate nutrients. Whether they reseed themselves depends upon the climate and conditions in which they are grown.

¶Perennial flowers, bulbs, and flowering shrubs and trees are extremely diverse, and generalizations about growing them are practically impossible to make. Many perennials may be grown from seed, but in the case of a tree or long-living shrub this can be a lengthy process. A number are standardly grown from vegetative cuttings. Vegetative reproduction is the process of forming independent plants from cuttings that are taken from desirable plants and induced to grow roots. Since all the original tissue of each cutting comes from one parent, it will be genetically identical to that parent. Shrubs, such as roses, lilacs, and gardenias, are commonly propagated this way. In the case of citrus, such as the dwarf kumquat, the cutting may be grafted onto rootstock for disease resistance or for faster flowering and fruiting.

¶Bulbs contain within themselves all that is needed to grow and flower within a year. Whether or not they repeat this process the following year depends, as with the self-seeding of annuals, on the conditions and climate in which they are grown.

¶Part of the pleasure of growing fragrant plants is seeking them out. Some of the most desirable types, such as rosa rugosa, alpine strawberry, 'Duchesse de Parma' violets, or 'Old Spice' sweet peas, once common, are now available only through nurseries or mail-order catalogues that specialize in the out of the ordinary. However, other fragrant flowers such as narcissus and hyacinths of all kinds, wisteria, lilacs, and gardenias are available from most nurseries, garden centers, and general mail-order garden catalogues.

¶Regardless of the source, starting with one- or two-year-old plants is recommended for shrubs and trees, and with seedlings or plant divisions for other perennials. Bulbs are the easiest fragrant flowers of all to grow, and since most annuals are easily grown from seeds, even the most intimidated novice should give growing these from scratch a try. It is quite a different experience to cover a seed or bulb with soil and then, one day, to see leaves emerging than it is to nurture an already growing plant.

Fragrant flowers, shrubs, and trees are so botanically and horticultur-ally diverse that a brief categoriza-tion for those included in this book is in order. This is followed by some general principles about their growing requirements.

SOIL, POTTING MIX, AND PREPARED GROUND

Soil is a mixture of the three soil particles, sand, silt, and clay, plus any organic matter. Sand is chemically inactive, so it is the clay and silt and the organic matter that are involved in the complex exchanges of water and plant nutrients. Sand, however, is by far the largest in size of the particles, so the presence of sand means that there will be correspondingly large spaces between soil particles. The very large soil pores that sand creates allow good drainage, high soil atmosphere concentrations, and good horizontal water movement.

¶The organic matter in soils is old plant material, decomposing under constant attack by bacteria and fungi. Over time these organisms liberate mineral elements that are essential to other plants for their growth.

¶An ideal soil would be composed of a mixture of sand, silt, clay, and organic matter in proportions that allow good drainage and aeration yet have adequate water- and nutrient-holding capabilities. A good loamy soil is about 60 percent sand, 20 percent silt, and 20 percent clay. Most soils are well under 5 percent organic matter. Commercial potting mixes are much, much higher in organic matter and much, much

Categories of Fragrant Flowers

To grow from seeds or seedlings
sweet pea: *annual*
heliotrope: *annual*
cottage pink: *perennial*
stock: *annual, may act as biennial*
alpine strawberry: *perennial*
datura: *annual, may act as biennial*

To grow from bulbs, pips, or tubers
tulip: *perennial, except in mild climates*
hyacinth: *perennial*
freesia: *perennial*
'Star Gazer' Asiatic lily: *perennial*
peony: *perennial*
lily-of-the-valley: *perennial*

To grow from young plants
trailing rosemary: *perennial*
scented-leaved geranium: *perennial*
dwarf kumquat tree: *tree*
sweet daphne: *shrub*
gardenia: *shrub*
English lavender: *perennial*
damask rose: *shrub*
sweet violet: *perennial*
wisteria: *vining shrub*
honeysuckle: *perennial vine*
poet's jasmine: *perennial vine*
rosa rugosa: *shrub*
lilac: *shrub*

lower in sand—more often than not containing no sand. The addition of sand to these mixes greatly increases the ease of ensuring adequate watering.

¶As healthy plants grow they extend roots through more and more of the surrounding soil. Consequently, higher percentages of sand and organic matter allow the plants to grow with less resistance than in heavy, closely packed soil. Furthermore the better drainage that greater amounts of sand and organic matter generally permit is critically important because the roots of many plants are susceptible to suffocating and rotting in soggy conditions.

¶To prepare ground for planting first remove existing plant material, such as plants you no longer want in the garden, or weeds. With a shovel, a spade, or a machine, such as a rototiller, turn the soil over to a depth of ten to twelve inches, adding sand and organic matter such as compost, rotted manure, or peat moss. Water once again and allow any undesirable seeds that may be in the ground to sprout. When the ground is dry enough to work, remove the newly germinated weeds and, using a hoe or shovel, break the soil up into small particles. The ground is now prepared for planting.

FERTILIZER

Generally commercial fertilizers list their contents as the percentage of each nutrient, in the order nitrogen-phosphorus-potassium, so a 20-10-10 fertilizer would be 20 percent nitrogen, 10 percent each phosphorus and potassium. A "balanced" fertilizer contains about equal parts of each major nutrient.

¶Nitrogen is the nutrient used most heavily in green vegetative growth, and it can be a determining factor in the usage of other nutrients. Phosphorus and potassium are

necessary for a wide range of plant functions, especially during periods of rapid growth, but they are closely linked to root and flower development.

¶Fertilizers come in many different forms, both dry and liquid. For most plants an all-purpose fertilizer, dry or liquid, adequately supplies nutrient needs, although for container plantings liquid fertilizers may be easier to apply.

¶A plant's needs for nutrients are greatest during periods of active growth, which are commonly in spring, or otherwise prior to flowering. To allow sufficient time for the fertilizer to break down in the soil, dissolve, and move into and throughout the plant, fertilize shortly before the growth period. Fertilizers that are applied many weeks or months ahead of this period may dissolve and percolate down and out of the root zone, and thus be lost to the plant at the time when they are needed.

Water

Plants need water to transport nutrients and complete photosynthesis, the energy-storing process. These two processes are so fundamental that water should always be available to the plants except during dormancy. A moist soil certainly makes water available, but a soggy soil can restrict growth or induce rotting by reducing the soil atmosphere. The amount of water needed by the plant varies with its stage of growth, with greater amounts needed when growth is greater.

¶Overwatering is a common source of plant loss. A moist soil does not necessarily have to be visibly wet on the surface but only moist in the root zone, where the plant utilizes it. The simplest way to determine if a soil is moist is to open it up with your finger or an implement and look at the soil in the root zone—is there water available to the roots? If so, don't water just to wet the top of the soil.

PESTS AND DISEASES

Plants are susceptible to an array of pests and diseases that vary by location. Obvious predators, like moles, gophers, and mice, can be readily detected, but very tiny insects, like bulb mites and thrips, are difficult to detect by those unfamiliar with their handiwork. There are various methods of control, and a local expert, such as a nurseryman, should be able to make informed suggestions to provide the most apt solution for your location.

FRAGRANT WINDOW BOXES AND PLANTERS

A fire escape, a windowsill, or a petit balcony can provide enough space for a potted garden brimming with colorful flowers and fragrant smells, evocative of mountains, forests, Elizabethan gardens, or of the mysterious tropics. Your container might be a classic window box attached outside your window or a wire-rack window box destined to hold pots. You might line up pots, round or rectangular, or use wooden crates, planting baskets, or any other planter that has good drainage. As long as you can provide one-half to two-thirds of a day of direct sunlight, even in the smallest apartment, a single terra-cotta pot planted with fragrant tulips or perhaps trailing rosemary will bring the sweet aromas of nature into your life. ❧ Both old-fashioned sweet peas, one of the most fragrant of all flowers, and heliotrope are easily grown from seed, even by a beginning gardener. Alpine strawberries, which are particularly treasured in Europe for the rich smell and taste of the tiny berries, adapt quite well to windowsill life. They, too, can be grown from seed. ❧ The short-lived but easily grown tulips, sweet peas, and heliotrope, along with the perennial alpine strawberry and rosemary, all bring distinctive fragrances to drift in on the air of an open window.

Fragrant sweet peas have a sweet, warmly clean clove and cinnamon scent like sheets that have been dried on a line in the early summer sun. However, not all sweet peas are fragrant, and it is not unusual to pick up a bouquet at a florist's, anticipating the flower's fragrance, only to find it scentless. ¶ For the distinctive sweet pea smell one must look to the older varieties, many of which are still available in England but somewhat difficult to find in this country. Unfortunately, most of the newer dwarf varieties, which are ideal for window boxes, do not have significant fragrance, so for fragrance you must choose a traditional vining type. Vining sweet peas grown in containers can be staked or trellised, but I like the rather wild, sensual look of the flowering vines twisting and curling from their container. ¶ For a container 24 inches long, 12 inches wide, and 10 inches deep you need 1 to 2 packets of seeds. Make sure the container has a hole in the bottom. Soak the seeds overnight in warm water. This allows each seed to fill itself with water and to start the growth process before it is planted. ¶ **HOW TO DO IT** ¶ For a container 24 inches long, 12 inches wide, and 10 inches deep you need 1 to 2 packets of seeds. Make sure the container has a hole in the bottom. Soak the seeds overnight in warm water. This allows each seed to fill itself with water and to start the growth process before it is planted. ¶ Cover the hole in the container with a little gravel, a few small rocks, or bits of broken pottery. Soak the potting mix with water until it is thoroughly moist, then fill the container with the mix to within ½ inch of the rim. Space the sweet pea seeds 2 inches apart, and with your fingertip, press them ½ inch deep into the potting mix, and cover. Pat the surface firmly. ¶ Place the container in a location that has at least one-half day of direct sun. Make sure the location is not so hot that it burns the emerging seedlings or, later, the plants. Keep the soil moist, and fertilize every three weeks with a liquid fertilizer. Remove dead leaves and blossoms.

Sweet Pea

Lathyrus odoratus 'Old Spice', 'Cuthbertson', 'Spencer'

❧

6 to 8 feet tall

Pink, rose, lavender, purple, magenta, burgundy, cream, white, or bicolor

❧

What You Need

1 to 2 packets seeds

Container at least 24 inches long, 12 inches wide, and 10 inches deep

Gravel, small rocks, or bits of broken pottery

Potting mix

Liquid fertilizer

Location with at least ½ day direct sun

❧

When to Buy

Fall or spring, from mail-order catalogue companies and specialty nurseries

❧

When to Plant

Fall in areas with hot summers; spring elsewhere

❧

Period of Bloom

About 80 days after planting, for 2 months

❧

Heliotrope's common name, cherry pie plant, gives you a clue to its scent, which has also been likened to vanilla, almonds, and cloves. A fixture in any Victorian garden or glasshouse of note, heliotrope was first brought to Europe from Peru in the 1750s and hybridized during the nineteenth century. Numerous hybrids exist today, some as small as 10 inches, others growing to more than 2 feet.

¶ Tall rampant plants need vigorous pruning to keep them looking their most luxuriant best, and any type that is grown with inadequate sunlight tends to become long and scraggly without ever blooming. Full, direct sun is needed to successfully grow heliotrope. All need plentiful watering during the warm summer.

¶ **HOW TO DO IT** ¶ Choose a container at least 12 inches in diameter and 8 inches deep. Make sure your container has a drainage hole in the bottom. Cover the hole with a little gravel, a few small rocks, or bits of broken pottery. ¶ Make a mixture of three-quarters potting mix and one-quarter sand. Soak the mixture with water until it is thoroughly moist, then fill the container with the mix to within ½ inch of the rim. Scatter the heliotrope seeds on the surface, ½ inch or so apart, and press them firmly into the soil mixture with the palm of your hand. Cover with ¼ inch moist potting mixture and pat smooth. ¶ Keep moist and in a warm location until germination occurs. This may take up to two weeks. Throughout the growing season keep the potting mixture moist, but not soggy. Fertilize once after about six weeks. Thin to six plants for small varieties and to two or three plants for larger ones. Remove dead leaves and flowers, and keep large plants pruned back.

Heliotrope
Heliotropium arborescens

❧

10 inches to 2 feet tall
Purple, lavender, or white

What You Need

❧

1 packet seeds
Container at least 12 inches in diameter and 8 inches deep
Gravel, small rocks, or bits of broken pottery
Potting mix
Sand
Small pruning clippers
Liquid fertilizer
Location with a full day direct sun

When to Buy

❧

Seeds, in early spring from mail-order catalogues or nurseries; plants, from early spring through early summer

When to Plant

❧

Seeds, in early spring, plants, from early spring through early summer

Period of Bloom

❧

Summer, for 2 months or longer

❧

Both the blossoms and the tiny, 1-inch-long fruits of this compact strawberry plant are richly perfumed. For me, the scent and taste is as if each perfect strawberry shortcake, pie, tart, ice cream, milk shake, and freshly gathered garden-patch berry of my experience were fused into a single intense explosion of the essence of strawberry. ¶ The alpine strawberry is everbearing, fruiting and blooming from spring through fall. Unlike the fraise de bois and today's hybrid strawberry plants, the alpine grows upright, rather than sending out runners, *which makes it ideal for window boxes and other small container plantings.* ¶ **HOW TO DO IT** ¶ For six alpine strawberry plants, choose a container at least 18 inches long and 10 inches deep. Make sure the container has a drainage hole in the bottom. Cover the hole with a little gravel, a few small rocks, or bits of broken pottery. Fill a bucket, pan, or sink full of water and then submerge the plants, still in their pots or trays, and let them stand until air bubbles cease to appear. While the plants are soaking, make a mixture of three-quarters potting mix and one-quarter sand. Soak the mixture with water until it is thoroughly moist, then fill the container to within ½ inch of the rim. Scoop out six holes 3 inches apart and approximately 4 inches deep. ¶ Gently remove the plants and their surrounding potting mix from their pots or trays and put them in the prepared holes. Fill in around their roots with the potting mixture and pat down the surface. Water to fill in any air pockets. ¶ Keep the potting mixture moist but not soggy. Fertilize the plants two weeks after potting, and approximately every two to three weeks thereafter as long as the plants continue to bloom and bear fruit. Remove dead leaves and stems.

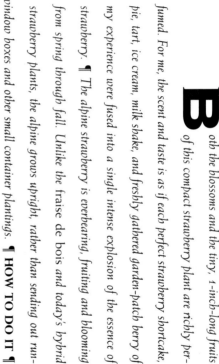

Alpine Strawberry
Fragaria vesca 'Alpine'

❊

10 to 12 inches tall

White flowers, red or yellow berries

What You Need

❊

6 plants

Container at least 12 inches in diameter and 8 inches deep

Gravel, small rocks, or bits of broken pottery

Potting mix

Sand

Liquid fertilizer

Location with ½ to ¾ day direct sun, or filtered sun in hot areas

When to Buy

❊

Early spring through midsummer, from nurseries and mail-order catalogues

When to Plant

❊

Early spring through midsummer

Period of Bloom

❊

Spring through fall, berries in spring through fall

❊

O nly a few tulips are fragrant, but those that are have a faintly sweet aroma that attracts without overwhelming, which adds yet another dimension of pleasure to an already wondrous flower. The fragrance is long lasting, enduring even as the spent blossoms begin to fold their petals back. ¶ Remarkable for their aesthetic versatility, tulips go through several stages. At first they look very stiff and soldierlike with the buds atop strong stems, and then the appearance begins to change as the tulips' cupping petals soften the soldier stance, and the stems bend toward the light source. My favorite stage, though, is when the flowers are spent, the petals bent back from the stamens, and the stems deeply waved and curved, as if exhausted from having supported the flower. All this and fragrance too make tulips an excellent choice for container planting, inside or out. ¶ Once planted and given adequate water, little other care is required, as the tulip bulbs contain all the nourishment needed to grow and bloom for one season. ¶ **HOW TO DO IT** ¶ For 12 bulbs, choose a container 10 inches in diameter and at least 12 inches deep with a hole in the bottom. Cover the hole with a little gravel, a few small rocks, or bits of broken pottery. Fill the container with potting mix to within 4 inches of the rim. Place the bulbs closely together, almost touching, on the mix, root sides down and pointed tips upward. Fill the container to within 1 inch of the rim with potting mix. Water to thoroughly saturate the mix. Put the container in a sunny location, and keep the potting mix moist until bloom has finished. ¶ If you live in an area with temperatures that drop below freezing, the bulbs may bloom again the following year. Let the leaves wither and die back after bloom and let the bulbs remain dry and undisturbed throughout the summer. In fall, fertilize with an all-purpose fertilizer. Few tulip varieties will repeat bloom in areas with warm winters, as most require a period of below-freezing temperatures.

Tulip

Tulipa: Single early, 'Bellona', 'General De Wet', double early, 'M. van der Hoeff', 'Triumph', 'Apricot Beauty', peony, 'Angelique'

10 to 16 inches

Various colors

❧

What You Need

12 bulbs

Container at least 10 inches in diameter and 12 inches deep

Gravel, small rocks, or bits of broken pottery

Potting mix

All-purpose fertilizer

Location with at least ½ day direct sun

❧

When to Buy

August through December from mail-order catalogues, September through January from nurseries and garden centers

❧

When to Plant

October through February

❧

Period of Bloom

Early spring to early summer, depending on variety, for several weeks

❧

TRAILING ROSEMARY

Rosemary

Rosmarinus officinalis

'Lockwood de Forest,' 'Prostratus'

6 to 8 inches tall

Dark to light blue, sometimes pink

❧

What You Need

4 plants (creeping types), 4-inch pot size

Container 24 inches long, 10 to 12 inches
wide, and at least 10 inches deep

Gravel, small rocks, or bits
of broken pottery

Potting mix

Sand

Small pruning clippers

Liquid fertilizer

Location with at least ½ day direct sun

❧

When to Buy

Spring through summer,
from nurseries and garden centers

❧

When to Plant

Spring through summer

❧

Period of Bloom

Winter and again in spring in
mild climates; spring and
early summer elsewhere

❧

The pungent, resinous fragrance of rosemary leaves and flowers is as welcome on a windowsill or balcony as it is in a simmering stew. One of the most significant of culinary herbs, rosemary is also an exceptional ornamental plant, particularly the trailing varieties, which form dark green cascades dotted with blue flowers when planted in containers. ¶ Rosemary is a sturdy, nearly indomitable plant when growing outside, but if kept inside in warm dry conditions, near a heater for example, or if it is overwatered, it loses its leaves and dies. If you can provide good drainage, direct sun, and circulating air your rosemary plants should flourish. ¶ **HOW TO DO IT** ¶ Submerge the rosemary plants, still in their purchased pots, in a bucket, pan, or sink full of water until air bubbles cease to appear. Choose a container about 24 inches long, 10 to 12 inches wide, and at least 10 inches deep. Make sure the container has a hole for drainage. Cover the hole with gravel, a few rocks, or bits of broken pottery. Make a mixture of three-quarters potting mix and one-quarter sand. Fill the container to within ½ inch of the rim. Soak the mixture with water. Scoop out four holes, each about 6 inches deep and 6 inches apart. ¶ Gently remove the rosemary plants from their pots, and examine their roots. If the roots go around and around the sides in the shape of the container, cut them back to the beginning of the circular growth. Now trim the top growth a like amount, so that it is in balance with the revised root system. For example, if you have trimmed away one-third of the root growth, you should trim an equal amount of top growth. ➔

¶ Put a plant in each hole and fill around the roots with moist potting mixture, packing well as you go. Water to fill in any air pockets. If possible, keep the plants outside or in an open window during the warm summer months. Water when the root zone is dry. Fertilize once a month from March through November with a fertilizer high in nitrogen, phosphorus, and potash. Prune growth back in winter to encourage strong spring and summer growth.

POTTED INDOOR FRAGRANCE

G rowing fragrant plants inside is ideal for the person who lacks outdoor garden space, but it should be considered not only as an alternative to an outdoor garden but as an extension of one. A number of delightfully scented and attractive plants, ranging from bulbs to shrubs to dwarf trees, flourish inside. ❦ Scented geraniums, many of which are native to South Africa, come in an array of floral, fruity, and spicy odors and perform especially well inside, season after season, if they are not overwatered. Hyacinths and freesias, spring-blooming bulbs, are good choices for short-lived intense, dizzying fragrance. ❦ More difficult to grow and maintain year after year are sweet daphne and dwarf citrus trees, but given solicitous care, these too will thrive in an indoor setting. Sweet daphne bursts open with pink and white blossoms, and the glossy green foliage of the kumquat tree becomes starred with tiny white blossoms, to be followed by the olive-shaped orange fruits. ❦ The greatest enemy for indoor plants is the moistureless air resulting from home heating and air conditioning, which can be as deadly inside as freezes can be outside. Provided light, circulating air, and appropriate moisture, fragrant plants in enclosed spaces with higher indoor temperatures reward the gardener with drifting aromas even more intense than they are outdoors.

Scented-leaved Geranium

Scented Pelargonium
(Scented-leaved Geranium)

Pelargonium graveolens,
P. citronellum, P. crispum, P. fragrans,
P. tomentosum, and hybrids

8 inches to 2 feet tall

Scented leaves are evergreen, insignificant
flowers are white, pink, or lavender

❦

What You Need

5 plants, 4-inch pot size

Container at least 18 inches in diameter
and 12 inches deep

Gravel, small rocks, or bits
of broken pottery

Potting mix

Sand

Geranium or all-purpose fertilizer

Location with ½ day or more of direct sun

❦

When to Buy

Year-round from nurseries and specialty
mail-order catalogues

❦

When to Plant
Year-round

❦

Period of Bloom
Intermittently year-round;
scent is year-round from leaves

❦

Scented pelargoniums, commonly called scented-leaved geraniums, imitate the fragrance of fruits, flowers, even of spices and herbs. Rub the leaves of the variety 'Fruit Punch' between your fingertips to release its volatile oils, close your eyes, and you would swear you were back at an eighth-grade dance lifting a cup of raspberry-pineapple Kool-Aid punch to your lips. First discovered in South Africa, the scented pelargoniums have become favorite houseplants because they thrive inside with little fussing, while they add a huge range of fragrance to the rooms. In addition, their leaves may be used for cooking and for making potpourri. ¶ An intriguing way to grow scented pelargoniums is to combine several different fragrance types in a single container. Not only the scents vary but also the growing habits and the colors and shapes of the leaves. Some leaves, for example those of the rose- and mint-scented geraniums, are ruffled and furred, while others, like the apple-scented, are bright green with faint white edges and are smooth to the touch. The white, pink, or lavender blossoms are the least striking feature of these plants, being small and not particularly perfumed. ¶ **HOW TO DO IT** ¶ Choose a container at least 18 inches in diameter and 12 inches deep. Make sure your container has a drainage hole in the bottom. Cover the hole with a little gravel, a few small rocks, or bits of broken pottery. Fill a bucket, pan, or sink with water. Submerge the geraniums, still in their purchased pots, in the water and let them stand until air bubbles cease to appear. While the plants are soaking, add sand to the potting mix to make a mixture that is one-third sand. Fill the planting container with the potting mixture to within ½ inch of the rim, and soak with water until the mixture is thoroughly moist. ¶ Remove the geraniums from ✒

their pots and gently shake off the potting mix around their roots. Scoop out a hole for each plant deep enough for the main root to extend straight down. Put a plant in each hole, gently fanning out the thin side roots, then fill in any empty spaces around the roots with the reserved soil. ¶ When the potting mix becomes dry at the depth of the roots, water the geraniums by submerging the entire container to soil level in water and letting it stand for at least half an hour or until the potting mix is saturated. Do not keep the potting mix perpetually soggy at root depth, as this condition may result in root rotting and plant death. ¶ Fertilize with a geranium or all-purpose fertilizer about once a month. Keep dead leaves removed, and to maintain, keep branches clipped back to the size you prefer.

HYACINTH

Hyacinth
Hyacinthus
8 to 10 inches tall
White, lavender, blue, violet, pink, salmon, or cream

❧

What You Need
1 bulb
Container at least 6 inches in diameter and 8 inches deep
Gravel, small rocks, or bits of broken pottery
Potting mix
Location with at least ½ to ½ day sun

❧

When to Buy
June through December from mail-order catalogues, August through December from nurseries

❧

When to Plant
December through March

❧

Period of Bloom
10 to 12 weeks after planting, for 2 to 3 weeks

❧

The hyacinth we most commonly see today, the Dutch hyacinth, is the result of centuries of hybridizing. Each bulb puts forth a fleshy stem that in time becomes three-quarters covered with a dense profusion of tiny colorful flowers. Hyacinth is native to the Mediterranean region, Asia minor, and Syria. When bulbs were gathered in the wild and brought back to Europe, plant breeders set to increasing the size and expanding the color range without diminishing the fragrance. ¶ *The hyacinth, with its singular, powerful fragrance, heavy, thick, and sweet, is the good luck symbol for the Zoroastrian New Year. Wherever members of this ancient Persian religion live, and many do live here in North America, giving one another potted hyacinths is a signifi-cant part of the New Year celebration, much as a New Year's custom among the Chinese is to give flowering quince and kumquat.* ¶ **HOW TO DO IT** ¶ For one hyacinth bulb, choose a con-tainer 6 inches wide and 8 inches deep with a hole in the bottom. Cover the bottom of the container with a layer of pebbles, gravel, or bits of broken pottery. Fill it half-full with moist potting mix. Place the bulb, root side down, pointed tip upward, on top of the mix. Cover with the potting mix, filling in the space between the bulb and container. Water thoroughly, allowing the potting mix to become saturated. ¶ Put the potted bulb in a dark place for three to four weeks—a closet or garage, for example—and water every week to ten days. The roots will grow during this time, and when you bring the hyacinth into the warmth and light of the house and the leaves and flowering spike start to grow, a strong root system will have developed to support the growth. ✦

Keep the growing hyacinth in a sunny location, maintaining the moisture until it blooms. To prolong the bloom, move the plant out of the direct sunlight. ¶ At the end of the blooming season, discard the spent bulb, as it will not produce good blooms again for a couple of seasons even with the best of care. ¶ Besides being planted in containers, hyacinths may be put in special glass hyacinth forcing jars or vases. These have short, narrow necks, or waists, where the bulb rests. The longer, lower portion of the jar is filled with water reaching just to the very bottom of the bulb. The roots grow down into the water, twisting and curling in full vision, while the bulb itself sits dry as it grows and blooms.

Dwarf Kumquat Tree

Kumquat blossoms have the clean, buoyant fragrance characteristic of citrus of all kinds. Like other citrus, kumquats are semitropical and cannot be successfully grown outdoors where extended freezes occur, but this fact did not keep intrepid Europeans living in cold climes from growing them. In royal courts from Russia to England, orangeries were designed solely to provide an environment in which citrus could flourish. ¶ Kumquats are one of the good luck symbols of Chinese New Year, and an indoor fruiting tree is considered to bring exceptional good luck in the forthcoming year. Trees are nurtured throughout the year to ensure fruit by January, when the month-long holiday begins. ¶ Kumquat trees flourish indoors as long as they have adequate water, fertilizer, and sunlight. Indoors, the greatest danger to the tree is not from freezes but from dryness caused by artificial heat or air conditioning. Dryness causes the trees to drop blossoms or fruit, and leaves as well. Keep the tree well-watered, which means a thorough watering approximately once a week, and fertilize it year-round. Kumquats bloom in summer and fall, and the fruit ripens in late winter through spring. ¶ **HOW TO DO IT** ¶ For a 5-gallon-pot-size tree, choose a container at least 18 inches across and 16 to 20 inches deep. Make sure the container has a drainage hole, preferably several, in the bottom. Cover the hole with a little gravel, a few small rocks, or bits of broken pottery. Make a mixture of two-thirds potting mix and one-third sand. Fill the container about one-third full of the mixture, and soak it with water until it is thoroughly moist. ¶ Fill a large bucket or sink with water and thoroughly soak the kumquat tree, still in its original pot, until the soil is saturated with water. Slip the tree, with as much soil as surrounds the root ball, out of the pot and into the container. Add moist ✒

Dwarf Kumquat

Fortunella margarita 'Nagami'

3 to 5 feet tall

White blossoms, orange fruit

❦

What You Need

5-gallon-pot-size plant

Container at least 18 inches in diameter and 20 inches deep

Gravel, small rocks, or bits of broken pottery

Potting mix

Sand

Balanced dry or liquid fertilizer

Location with at least ½ day full sun

❦

When to Buy

September through March, from nurseries

❦

When to Plant

September through April

❦

Period of Bloom

Summer, for several weeks or more, fruits appear in winter or early spring

❦

potting mixture, packing it firmly around the root ball. The graft of the tree (you will see a scar or band several inches above the root base) should be well above the soil level. The rim of the container should be 2 to 3 inches above the soil level. ¶ Scatter a dry balanced fertilizer atop the soil and water, or use a liquid fertilizer. Water again in two days and every week thereafter, or more often if necessary. Do not let the soil dry out. Fertilize every four weeks. ¶ Keep your kumquat tree indoors in a location that gets at least one-half day of direct sun. In temperate seasons the kumquat tree may be moved outside, but give it an adjustment period first, as radical environmental changes can be harmful to it. For example, when you move it outside, place it in the shade for several days before moving it to a sunny location.

I was once given a nosegay of flowers that included freesias, and for several days I took the nosegay

and its vase with me from room to room, reluctant to leave the fragrance.

During the day I kept it on my desk on the sunporch, where the warmth of the thin spring sun coming through the glass heated the flowers and released their scent. In the evening I moved the bouquet into the kitchen, where its honeyed citruslike perfume mingled harmoniously with whatever I cooked.

At the end of each day I tucked the bouquet near my bedside reading lamp, and there it continued to scent the air with its intense, clean smell of spice. ¶ Happily, freesias, which grow from bulbs, may easily be raised inside in containers. They return to bloom year after year provided they have cool temperatures, such as on an unheated porch, and adequate light and humidity. ¶ **HOW TO DO IT** ¶ For 18 bulbs, choose a container 18 inches in diameter and at least 10 inches deep with a hole in the bottom. Cover the hole with a little gravel, a few small rocks, or bits of broken pottery. ¶ Fill the container to within 4 inches of the rim with moist potting mix. Place the bulbs 2 inches apart, root side down, pointed tips upward, on the surface of the mix. Cover with moist potting mix to within 1 inch of the rim. ¶ Keep the container in a sunny location where nighttime temperatures are cool. Keep potting mix moist but not soggy. After the bulbs have sprouted, fertilize monthly with a dilute solution of liquid fertilizer. If flower stalks threaten to fall over, carefully insert stakes at an angle, so as not to damage bulbs or roots, and tie the stalks to the stakes. ¶ Freesias may be left in the same container for several years. When their bloom is over, reduce watering, allowing the foliage to yellow and wither. Start watering again in the fall.

Freesia
Freesia

12 to 18 inches tall

White, pinks, reds, blues, yellows, or purples

❧ What You Need

18 bulbs

Container 18 inches in diameter and at least 10 inches deep

Gravel, small rocks, or bits of broken pottery

Potting mix

Liquid fertilizer

Stakes (if needed)

Location with at least ½ day direct sun

❧ When to Buy

July through October from mail-order catalogues; September through January from nurseries

❧ When to Plant

September through January

❧ Period of Bloom

3 to 4 months after planting, for 1 month or longer

❧

Sweet Daphne

Sweet Daphne
Daphne odora
4 to 6 feet tall
Whitish pink

❧

What You Need

1 plant, 1-gallon-can size
Container at least 18 inches in diameter
and 12 inches deep, preferably terra-cotta
Gravel, rocks, or bits of broken pottery
Potting mix
Sand
Small pruning clippers
Liquid fertilizer
Location with ½ day direct sun
or ½ day filtered sun

❧

When to Buy
Fall

❧

When to Plant
Fall

❧

Period of Bloom
December through spring,
for several months

❧

My initial experience with sweet daphne was about ten years ago at the home of an elderly and gifted gardener. As we walked around her garden on a cold March morning, she plucked a rather nondescript little cluster of flowers and leaves and tucked it into the buttonhole of my jacket. What a scent! It rose up from beneath my chin, enveloping me in a wall of pure sweet fragrance. I wanted to wear that boutonniere forever, and use no other perfume, so much was I taken by it. ¶ Daphne performs well indoors in containers and will bloom in December given the right conditions. Temperatures should be cool with nights no more than 40 degrees F, and not much warmer than that during the daytime. An unheated porch is ideal. The daphne's roots are quick to rot, so potting should be in a sandy mix that will allow good root drainage. Terra-cotta containers are a good choice because they are porous and thus facilitate drainage. Overwatering is sure death to a daphne, as is too much sun. This is a tricky plant to grow, but the fragrance it offers makes the effort worthwhile. ¶ **HOW TO DO IT** ¶ For a 1-gallon-can-size sweet daphne you need a container 18 inches in diameter and 12 inches deep, preferably terra-cotta. Make sure your container has a drainage hole in the bottom. Cover the hole with a little gravel, a few small rocks, or bits of broken pottery. ¶ Make a mixture of two-thirds potting mix and one-third sand. Fill your container about half-full of the mixture and soak the mix until it is thoroughly moist. Fill a bucket, pan, or sink with water and submerge the plant, still in its pot. Let it stand until air bubbles cease to emerge. Remove the plant from its can and examine the roots. If they go around and around at the sides in the shape of the can, cut them back to the beginning of the ❧

circular growth. Trim the top growth a like amount so that it is in balance with the revised root system. For example, if you clip back one-third of the roots, clip back also one-third of the plant's top growth. ¶ Hold your plant upright in the half-full container and fill around the roots with moist potting mix, packing well as you go. Fill to within ½ inch of the rim. Pat down the surface, and water to fill in any air pockets. ¶ Water only when the soil mix is dry in the root-zone area. Soggy wet soil is far more harmful to a daphne than a slightly dry soil. Fertilize once a year, after bloom is finished. Repot to a larger pot when the plant is one-and-a-half times to twice its original size.

OUTDOOR
MOVABLE
FRAGRANCE

Fragrant plants potted in containers are an obvious solution for someone who has no garden ground or who lives in a climate with formidable winters. Containers can be moved into protected areas for overwintering and brought back outside when the weather warms. Whether the climate is temperate or harsh, outdoor potted plants have a place in the garden, and this is especially true of fragrant plants. Because they are in movable containers they can be placed under a bedroom window, or moved near an outdoor table or rocking chair, so that the fragrance follows the sensory whims and desires of the possessor. ✳ The long, narrow, overhung porches of southern California's ranch-style houses become corridors of tropical fragrance when lined with terra-cotta jars or wooden boxes brimming with waxy white gardenia blossoms. Daturas, potted and arching their sensuous, richly scented trumpet flowers are a constant reminder of the exotic Asian climes of the flower's origin. ✳ Damask roses, the perfumer's choice for scent manufacturing, surround their containers with near-tangible clouds of essence of rose. Along with the massively honey-and-almond scented 'Star Gazer' lilies, they join gardenias and daturas to make moveable feasts of fragrance.

L ong, downward-facing trumpets of palest cream grow on shrubby plants that may reach a height of 2 feet. The trumpets themselves are about 8 inches long, and they open in the late afternoon and early evening to infuse the air around them with a fine, honeyed fragrance. This fragrant and quite beautiful ornamental datura is a native of southwestern China, but other daturas, notably the foetid-smelling jimson weed, are native American plants. All daturas are sources of alkaloids, and the leaves and seeds are poisonous if eaten. ¶ The datura is a popular decorative potted plant in Europe because of its fragrance, rapid growing habit, and unusual shape. The datura, like the calla lily, was a favorite subject of art nouveau graphics, and its shape is found etched in glass windows, painted onto porcelain plates, cast into bronze lamp bases, and repeated as a motif on other ornaments of the era. ¶ **HOW TO DO IT** ¶ For a single specimen plant, choose a container 18 inches in diameter and 18 inches deep with a hole in the bottom. Cover the hole with a little gravel, a few small rocks, or bits of broken pottery. Fill the container to within 2 inches of the rim with the potting mix. Soak the mix until it is thoroughly moist. ¶ Plant the seeds 6 inches apart and ¼ inch deep, covering them with moist potting mix. Keep the mix moist until germination occurs and then water regularly thereafter. When the seedlings have six leaves, thin out all except the two strongest-looking ones. Fertilize every six weeks with an all-purpose liquid fertilizer. Plants will endure until the first heavy frost. ¶ In areas with late frost the seeds may be started indoors, and the seedlings then moved outside when temperatures have warmed and there is no longer any danger of frost.

Datura
Datura metel
1 to 2 feet tall
White to cream with purplish pink tinge

❧
What You Need
8 to 10 seeds
Container at least 18 inches in diameter
and 18 inches deep
Gravel, small pebbles, or bits
of broken pottery
Potting mix
All-purpose liquid fertilizer
Location with at least ½ day direct sun

❧
When to Buy
Winter through spring, from specialty
mail-order catalogues

❧
When to Plant
Early spring

❧
Period of Bloom
14 to 15 weeks after planting seeds,
lasting for several months

❧

GARDENIA

What You Need

5-gallon-pot-size plant

Container at least 18 inches in diameter and 24 inches deep

Gravel, small rocks, or bits of broken pottery

Potting mix of at least ½ peat moss

Small pruning clippers

Bloodmeal or fish-emulsion fertilizer

Location with full sun in moderate temperatures or filtered sun in high temperatures

When to Buy

Spring

When to Plant

Spring

Period of Bloom

Late spring or early summer, for 5 to 6 months

Gardenias have a torrid, moist-earth scent that *some people find overwhelming, but that I personally love. As a child in southern California in the late 1940s and 1950s, I watched my mother and her friends tuck gardenias behind their ears for beach parties, and I well remember my father coming home with a lei of gardenias he had had specially made for a dance he took my mother to that evening.* ¶ Given the right combination of soil mixture, temperature, and water, gardenias flourish in containers. They are unforgiving of growing conditions beyond the narrow range that they require, but the reward for providing it is dozens of waxy white blossoms, which permeate the air around them with a deep, heady, unduplicatable fragrance. ¶ **HOW TO DO IT** ¶ For a 5-gallon-pot-size gardenia plant, choose a container at least 18 inches across and 24 inches deep with a hole in the bottom. Cover the bottom with a layer of gravel, small rocks, or bits of broken pottery. Make a mixture of two-thirds potting mix and one-third peat moss, or use a purchased mixture that is one-third peat moss. Fill the container approximately one-half full with the mixture and water thoroughly to soak. Meanwhile, fill a large bucket or sink with water and soak the gardenia plant, still in its pot, until saturated and air bubbles no longer emerge. ¶ Gently remove the plant from its pot, shaking loose the soil. Examine the roots. If they go around and around the sides in the shape of the pot, cut them back to the beginning of the circular growth. Now trim the top growth a like amount, so that it is in balance with the revised root system. For example, if you have trimmed away one-third of root growth you should trim an equal amount of top growth. Hold the plant upright in the container, and pack the roots with moist potting mixture, filling the container to within 2 to 3 inches of the rim but being careful to plant the gardenia ✒

no deeper than the previous potting line. ¶ Gardenias need summer heat to bloom well and should be in full sun except in areas with high summer temperatures, where the container should be placed in a location that receives filtered sunlight. Fertilize every three to four weeks from early spring through late fall with an acidic fertilizer, bloodmeal, or fish emulsion. Always keep the soil moist and remove dead leaves and blossoms.

Interveinal yellowing of younger leaves, common in gardenias, is called chlorosis, and it usually indicates an iron deficiency. The treatment is an application of chelated iron (iron that is readily soluble and accessible to the plant), either in granular form or as a foliar spray. This is commonly found in garden centers and nurseries. ¶ In areas where winter temperatures drop below 30 degrees, overwinter gardenias in a sheltered location.

Lavender is one of the classic perfume scents, and over the centuries flowers have been distilled to make lavender oil, essence of lavender, and perfume. In many households in and around the Alpes d'Haute Provence, where the high plateaus are covered with commercial acres of undulating waves of the deep purple flowers, people add drops of lavender oil to the water in their cleaning buckets. When the red tile floors have been thoroughly mopped, the rooms have the resinous sweet scent of the lavender fields themselves. ¶ Lavender adapts readily to container growing and it is quite hardy, capable of withstanding freezing temperatures.

¶ HOW TO DO IT ¶ For a 1-gallon-pot-size plant, choose a container at least 12 inches in diameter and 24 to 36 inches deep with a drainage hole in the bottom. Put a 10-inch layer of gravel or other rocks on the bottom to served as a drainage layer. Make a mixture of two-thirds potting mix and one-third sand. Fill the container to within 2 inches of the top with the mixture and soak it until thoroughly moist. Scoop out a hole large enough for the roots of the lavender plant. ¶ Submerge the lavender plant, still in its original pot, in a large bucket or sink full of water until air bubbles cease to appear. Gently remove the plant from its pot and examine its roots. If the roots curl around and around in the shape of the pot, cut them back to the beginning of the circular growth. Trim the top growth a like amount so that it is in balance with the revised root system. For example, if you clip back one-third of the roots, clip back also one-third of the top growth. ¶ Put the lavender plant in the prepared container and fill around the roots with the potting mixture, patting down the surface. Water again to fill in any air pockets. ¶ Fertilize your lavender plant in spring and cut off old stems in the fall. Water as needed, but do not allow the soil mix to stay soggy, as lavender requires good drainage.

English Lavender
Lavandula angustifolia
2 to 3 feet tall
Purple to lavender

❈

What You Need
1-gallon-pot-size plant
Container at least 12 inches in diameter and 24 to 36 inches deep
Gravel or small rocks
Potting mix
Sand
Small pruning clippers
Liquid or other fertilizer
Location with ½ to a full day direct sun

❈

When to Buy
When plants are still dormant or show new growth but have not yet bloomed

❈

When to Plant
Early spring through summer before bloom appears

❈

Period of Bloom
Late spring through midsummer, sometimes with second bloom in fall, for a month or longer

❈

'STAR GAZER' ASIATIC LILY

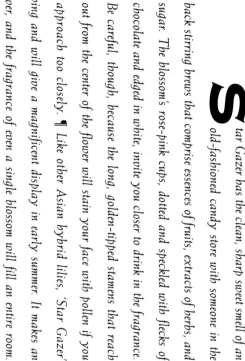

Star Gazer has the clean, sharp sweet smell of an old-fashioned candy store with someone in the back stirring brews that comprise essences of fruits, extracts of herbs, and sugar. The blossom's rose-pink cups, dotted and speckled with flecks of chocolate and edged in white, invite you closer to drink in the fragrance. Be careful, though, because the long, golden-tipped stamens that reach out from the center of the flower will stain your face with pollen if you approach too closely. ¶ Like other Asian hybrid lilies, 'Star Gazer' adapts well to container growing and will give a magnificent display in early summer. It makes an excellent, long-lasting cut flower, and the fragrance of even a single blossom will fill an entire room.

¶ HOW TO DO IT ¶ For three bulbs, choose a container at least 18 inches in diameter and 18 inches deep with a hole in the bottom. Cover the hole with a little gravel, a few small rocks, or bits of broken pottery. Make a mixture of three-quarters potting mix and one-quarter well-rotted manure. Soak it thoroughly, then fill the container to within 2 inches of the rim with the mixture. ¶ Scoop out three holes about 5 inches deep. Place a bulb root side down in each hole. The top of the bulb should be no more than 2 inches below the surface. Cover with moist potting mix and put the container in a cool place. ¶ Keep the potting mix moist but not soggy, and keep it watered during and after the blooming period. When shoots appear, move the container to a location where there is a half-day or more of direct sun, or of filtered sun in hot summer areas. Temperatures consistently above 90 degrees inhibit growth and bloom. With the onset of winter, protect with mulch or move container to a protected location.

Asiatic Lily
Lilium Asiatic hybrid 'Star Gazer'

3 to 5 feet tall

Rose-pink speckled with chocolate, white edges

❧

What You Need

3 bulbs

Container at least 18 inches in diameter and 18 inches deep

Gravel, small rocks, or bits of broken pottery

Potting mix

Well-rotted manure

All-purpose fertilizer

Location with full sun in moderate temperatures or filtered sun in high temperatures

❧

When to Buy

September through March from mail-order catalogues; January through March from nurseries

❧

When to Plant

September and October or March through May

❧

Period of Bloom

Summer into fall, for about 6 weeks

❧

DAMASK ROSE

Damask Rose

Rosa damascena and hybrids

5 feet tall

White, cream, rose, pink, or violet, solid or striped

❋

What You Need

1- or 2-year-old plant, bare root

Container at least 24 inches in diameter and 24 inches deep

Gravel, small rocks, or bits of broken pottery

Potting mix

Sand

Peat moss

Small pruning clippers

Rose or all-purpose fertilizer

Location with ½ or ⅔ day direct sun

❋

When to Buy

Late fall, winter, or early spring

❋

When to Plant

Winter in mild winter areas, early spring elsewhere

❋

Period of Bloom

Late spring, summer, or sometimes fall, for several weeks

❋

I n Bulgaria's Valley of the Roses, located near the town of Kazanluk in central Bulgaria, hundreds of thousands of damask rose blossoms are hand-harvested from thorny, arching branches to produce the world's finest, most expensive, most sought after attar of roses—rose oil—for use in the perfume industry. For hundreds of years, traders in rose oil have come to the Valley of the Roses to examine the results of the harvest and to bargain with the producers. ¶ The damask rose was most likely brought back to Europe during the Middle Ages by crusaders returning from the Levant, where the damask had long been known and treasured. There are numerous varieties of damask roses and their hybrids, although they are no longer as common as they once were. They and their hybrids exist in myriad colors, sizes, and forms, and while all are noteworthy for their fragrance, many of the older varieties bloom only once a year. For repeat bloom, look for so-called autumn damasks or damask hybrids. ¶ Like other roses, the damask is best planted when it is dormant. This allows new growth to begin after the transplanting and avoids transplanting shock. Often dormant roses are sold bare root, which means without soil adhering to the roots. ¶ **HOW TO DO IT** ¶ For a two-year-old bare-root damask rose, you will need a container at least 24 inches in diameter and 24 inches deep. Make sure your container has a drainage hole in the bottom. Cover the hole in the container with a little gravel, a few small rocks, or bits of broken pottery. Fill the container about one-quarter full with a moist potting mixture that contains at least one-third sand and one-third peat moss. ¶ Soak the roots of the rose overnight in a large bucket or sink full of water. Remove the rose from the water and trim the roots, removing any that are broken or dead. Hold the plant upright in the container and fill around the roots with the moist potting mixture, packing well as you go, leaving 4 or 5 inches to the rim to allow ➹

for watering. Adjust planting height if necessary. Water thoroughly to saturate the potting mixture. ¶ Place the container in a location that receives one-half to three-quarters of a day of direct sun, but keep it away from the intense, reflected heat of walls, which can burn the leaves. ¶ Keep the soil moist throughout the growing season, watering more during hot summer weather. Fertilize weekly with rose or all-purpose fertilizer. Pruning is best done in the winter when the plant is dormant. There is no need to overwinter inside or in a protected location, as the damask rose is extremely hardy.

Walking along a path swathed in a cloud of fragrance is a sensual and intoxicating experience, particularly on warm days when the essential oil from the flowers is volatilized by the sun's warmth. Each brush of a hand, trailing skirt, or trouser cuff releases an intense burst of fragrance into the already perfumed air ✻ To border a walkway with clumps of perfumed flowers, there are numerous plants from which to choose. Lily-of-the-valley, the tiny bell-shaped flower that is a classic symbol of spring and bridal bouquets, with its airy, light scent and glistening sword-shaped leaves, makes an inviting border to a shady path. Combinations of long-blooming clove-scented cottage pinks and sweet old-fashioned stocks are reminiscent of turn of the century cottage gardens. In late winter and early spring when rain and mud keep us from wandering into the garden proper, narcissus, one of the earliest-blooming bulbs, is always in reach if planted along a frequented path. Sweet violets are highly resilient and can be planted overlapping the edges of the path or tucked between the bricks or stones of the pathway itself, where each footstep will release the flowers' sweet smell ✻ Even if the only path available to you is from the street to the front door, or along the side of the apartment, that is enough space to fill with fragrance.

I love the old-fashioned name for these—sops in wine—so called because they were used to flavor wine. As long ago as the seventeenth century, these small flowers smelling of clove were garden favorites, and they figure in descriptions of gardens of that era along walkways, in beds, and potted. Hugely popular, the cottage pinks and their relatives, the carnations and other members of the dianthus tribe, were crossed with one another to create new types and new varieties both for the floral industries and the garden. ¶ Differing from the basic cottage pink, which had only five fringed petals and was actually white or pale pink, today's cottage pinks generally have frilled double petals, and their colors are a riot of bright pink, burgundy, white and pastels, and combinations thereof. The characteristic rich clove scent of the original remains.

¶ **HOW TO DO IT** ¶ To fill a 10-foot-by-1-foot space along a walkway you need thirty to forty seeds. Plant the seeds ⅛ inch deep and about 6 inches apart in thoroughly moist, prepared soil in a location that receives at least a half-day of sun. Keep the soil moist until germination occurs, which may be as late as three weeks after sowing the seeds. Water as needed thereafter. ¶ Once the plants have formed buds, reduce the watering. To ensure continuous bloom, remove dead flowers.

Cottage Pink
Dianthus plumarius

1 to 1½ feet tall

Dark pink, burgundy, white, pastels, or bicolored

❋

What You Need

1 packet seeds

10 square feet of prepared ground with at least ½ day full sun

❋

When to Buy

December through March, from mail-order catalogues and some nurseries

❋

When to Plant

Early spring, for bloom the first year

❋

Period of Bloom

Summer, for 2 to 3 months

❋

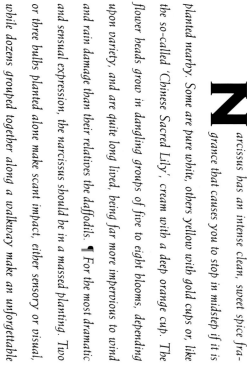

Narcissus has an intense clean, sweet spice fragrance that causes you to stop in midstep if it is planted nearby. Some are pure white, others yellow with gold caps or, like the so-called 'Chinese Sacred Lily', cream with a deep orange cup. The flower heads grow in dangling groups of five to eight blooms, depending upon variety, and are quite long lived, being far more impervious to wind and rain damage than their relatives the daffodils. ¶ For the most dramatic and sensual expression, the narcissus should be in a massed planting. Two or three bulbs planted alone make scant impact, either sensory or visual, while dozens grouped together along a walkway make an unforgettable spring tableau. ¶ Narcissus naturalizes, producing more bulbs and thus an increased bloom each year. However, in order to do this the bulb draws upon the nutrients in its dying leaves to restore its resources, and so the leaves must be left to wither and brown before removing them. ¶ **HOW TO DO IT** ¶ To fill a 6-foot-by-2-foot space along a walkway you need approximately fifty bulbs. Plant the bulbs 6 inches deep, root sides down and points upward, 2 to 4 inches apart. The closer together they are planted the more solid the first year's bloom will appear. After planting, water thoroughly to saturate the soil. ¶ When the narcissus are through blooming, snap off any remaining flower heads and let the leaves grow until they wither and brown. The leaves may then be cut back or left to die. Fertilize in fall with a balanced fertilizer.

Narcissus
Narcissus tazetta
12 to 16 inches tall
White, yellow, or white and orange

❦

What You Need
50 bulbs
Balanced fertilizer
12 square feet of prepared ground
with at least ½ day full sun

❦

When to Buy
June through October from
mail-order catalogues; September
through January from nurseries

❦

When to Plant
October through January

❦

Period of Bloom
Winter through spring,
for a month or longer

❦

Stock's spiked stems are covered with dozens of double flowers in compelling shades of purple, lavender, maroon, and white. Single-flowered varieties exist as well, but the doubles, whether they are dwarf or tall types, are notably more fragrant, releasing a sweet clovelike perfume. ¶ Native to the hills and cliffs of southern England and Europe, stock was popular with English and European flower breeders as early as the sixteenth century. Numerous strains of stock that exist today were bred from the scraggly yet perfumed wild plant, including the one called ten-week, a modern and very popular type for the obvious reason—it blooms ten weeks from sowing. ¶ Stock is a faint bloomer when the weather becomes hot, but it will bloom profusely in cool weather. In mild climates that have little or no frost over winter, stock blooms from fall through winter and into early spring. In areas with frost and freezes, stock is an early-summer flowerer. I have found that where I live in California stock is almost indestructible, coming back to flower in places I have forgotten I planted it. ¶ **HOW TO DO IT** ¶ To fill a space along a walkway 8 feet by 4 feet, you need approximately 2 packets of seeds. Plant the seeds 12 inches apart and cover with a scant ⅛ inch of soil or vermiculite. Stock seeds need light to germinate. ¶ Keep the soil moist until germination occurs, generally within seven days to two weeks, and keep adequately watered thereafter. The roots are subject to rot, so do not overwater the plants.

Stock

Matthiola incana
8 inches to 2 feet tall
Pastels, burgundy, purple,
dark pink, white, or bicolor

❧

What You Need
2 packets seeds
Vermiculite, if used
32 square feet of prepared ground
with at least ½ day full sun

❧

When to Buy
Year-round from mail-order
catalogues and nurseries

❧

When to Plant
Mid to late summer in mild climates;
early spring elsewhere

❧

Period of Bloom
Fall through early spring in mild climates
late spring through midsummer elsewhere

❧

SWEET VIOLET

Nosegays of violets were de rigueur for female theatre-goers at the turn of the century, much as corsages of gardenias or orchids were during the 1940s. Although women were warned against whiffing too long of the sweet violet's dizzying aroma, they nevertheless inhaled deeply of the tiny bouquets they held in their hands, risking, according to some, "losing their heads."

¶ Josephine de Beauharnais, the widowed Creole from Martinique who was Napoleon Bonaparte's great love, entertained no fear of her favorite flower. She surrounded herself with violets, and its design was even part of the motif in the Bonaparte coat of arms. ¶ Of the modern, commercially grown strains of sweet violet, few are truly fragrant. For the intense sweetness for which violets are famous, you must locate one of the old-fashioned, still-fragrant strains listed below. ¶ **HOW TO DO IT** ¶ To fill a 12-by-2-foot space along a walkway you need 48 violet plants. Fill a large bucket or sink full of water and submerge the plants, still in their pots, until air bubbles cease to appear. In prepared, thoroughly moist garden soil, dig holes one and a half times as deep and as wide as the violet pots. Space the holes about 6 inches apart. ¶ Gently remove the violet plants from their pots, along with their potting mix, and put one in each prepared hole. Fill the hole with moist soil and pat the surface firmly around the roots. Water to fill in any air pockets. ¶ Keep the soil moist, especially during blooming season. The plants will begin to die back during the hot summer months and will go dormant during winter. Cover in winter with a layer of dead leaves or other mulch. Fertilize in spring after the first new leaves have appeared. After several years, dig them up and divide and replant them.

Sweet Violet

Viola odorata 'The Czar', 'Queen Charlotte'

8 to 12 inches tall

Purple, lavender, blue, or rose-pink

❧

What You Need

48 plants

Fertilizer

24 square feet of prepared ground with at least ½ day full sun

❧

When to Buy

Early spring, from nurseries and specialty mail-order catalogues

❧

When to Plant

Early spring through early summer

❧

Period of Bloom

Late winter and early spring, for 2 to 3 months

❧

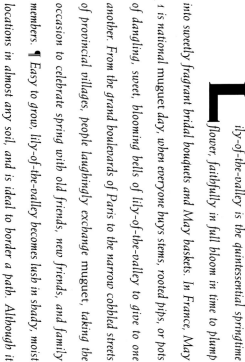

Lily-of-the-valley is the quintessential springtime flower, faithfully in full bloom in time to plump into sweetly fragrant bridal bouquets and May baskets. In France, May 1 is national muguet day, when everyone buys stems, rooted pips, or pots of dangling, sweet, blooming bells of lily-of-the-valley to give to one another. From the grand boulevards of Paris to the narrow cobbled streets of provincial villages, people laughingly exchange muguet, taking the occasion to celebrate spring with old friends, new friends, and family members. ¶ Easy to grow, lily-of-the-valley becomes lush in shady, moist locations in almost any soil, and is ideal to border a path. Although it blooms for only a short period in spring, it puts forth shiny deep green ground cover from early spring until frozen back by the winter cold. ¶ **HOW TO DO IT** ¶ To fill a 2-by-6-foot space along a walkway, you need 72 pips. Plant the pips 4 inches apart and 1 inch deep. Place one pip in each hole. Cover with soil and pat the surface firmly. Water thoroughly to saturate the soil. ¶ Keep plants well watered throughout the growing season. In areas with cold winters, mulch them in the fall for protection. In mild-winter areas, no protection is necessary. Fertilize in late fall.

Lily-of-the-valley
Convallaria majalis
8 to 10 inches tall

White

❋

What You Need

72 pips

Fertilizer

12 square feet of prepared ground
in shade or partial shade

❋

When to Buy

September through March from nurseries
and from mail-order catalogues

❋

When to Plant

September through March in mild-winter
areas; September through October elsewhere

❋

Period of Bloom

May and June, and sometimes
April, for several weeks

❋

BOWERS AND
HEDGES OF
FRAGRANCE

ne of the most dramatic and sensual settings for fragrant flowers is a bower or hedge. In bowers, twisting vines, sometimes combined with trees for additional height

or support, create a garden refuge. Within the bower, slightly enclosed from the rest of the garden, the fragrance from the flowers is trapped to some extent, and fills the bower space with the flower's volatilizing oils. Wisteria, honeysuckle, and poet's jasmine are all climbing, sinuous vines that can be relied upon to deliver sweet smells. ❧ Hedges of perfume, perhaps of old-fashioned peonies or the classic single-petaled rosa rugosa, invite lingering wherever they are planted. On warm days especially, don't resist the temptation to pause and imbibe the sweetness emanating from the hedge, or the temptation to pick a few blooms and bring the fragrance along with you into the house. ❧ Sweet-scented bowers and hedges have no particular growing requirements other than those determined by your space, sunlight, and garden location. However, bowers and sometimes hedges frequently need support and pruning to shape them according to your vision. ❧ Supports can be as simple as strands of galvanized metal wire anchored to the ground and a nearby tree, or they can be purchased ready-made in wood or cast iron as trellises or arches. Custom construction of arbors, trellises, or other support structures in wood or metal opens vast possibilities for individual design and expression. ❧ Skillful pruning is considered to be an art form, but even a novice can master the basic technique of removing dead wood, clipping branches or shoots back to encourage new growth, and cutting back overly rampant growth.

When standing beneath a gossamer ceiling of wisteria vines in full bloom, engulfed by the

delicate enticing fragrance, one's scent and sight seem to fuse into a single sense. Wisteria is particularly well-suited to bowers because it has woody trunks and roping vines that need only minimal support to create massed clusters of overhanging flowers, some as long as 2 feet, that develop in the warmth of late spring. ¶ *Remarkably hardy, wisteria can be grown with little difficulty in almost any climate.*

¶ HOW TO DO IT ¶ For a 2-year-old plant in a 5-gallon pot, you need approximately 10 square feet of prepared garden ground in a location that receives full sun. Dig a hole 2 feet deep and 2 feet in diameter. ¶ Fill a large bucket or sink full of water. Submerge the plant, still in its original container, in the water until no further air bubbles appear. Remove the wisteria from its pot and gently brush away the soil to examine the roots. If the roots go around and around the sides in the shape of the container, cut them back to the beginning of the circular growth. Now trim the top growth a like amount, so that it is in balance with the revised root system. For example, if you have trimmed away one-third of the root growth, you should trim an equal amount of top growth. Hold the plant upright in the hole and fill in around the roots, packing the soil around them. The uppermost portion of the roots should be just below the surface, which should meet the preexisting soil line on the trunk. Place the trellis, wires, or other support approximately 10 inches away from the plant. ¶ Water throughout the early growth and bloom, and fertilize with an all-purpose fertilizer every four weeks. When the leaves have dried and dropped in early winter, prune back the flowering shoots, leaving only 2 or 3 inches.

Wisteria
Wisteria sinensis,
W. floribunda

10 to 20 feet or more tall

Lavender, white, blue-violet, violet, or pink

❧

What You Need

2-year-old-plant, 5-gallon-pot size

Small pruning shears

All-purpose fertilizer

10 square feet of prepared ground with full sun

❧

When to Buy

Spring, from nurseries

❧

When to Plant

Spring

❧

Period of Bloom

Late spring or early summer, for 4 to 6 weeks

❧

A hedge of rosa rugosa is far more formidable than barbed wire and unquestionably more beautiful

and fragrant. I still imagine the thorny hedge around Sleeping Beauty's castle as rosa rugosas. ¶ I have about eighty of the species planted along my drive, and the perfume from them is obvious when I walk by on a warm spring evening. If kept watered they bloom three-quarters of the year, ceasing only in full winter with the onset of frosts. Even then the large, bright hips remain, which I cut for winter bouquets. When I do, I bring out the elbow-high garden gloves as well as the clippers, because the stems of these lovely roses are solid thorns. Every inch, even every quarter inch is thick with the sharp barbs. ¶ Rosa rugosa is perhaps the sturdiest of all roses, thriving and blooming everywhere, virtually unaffected by disease or predatory insects. From year-old bare-root plants you can expect a 4- to 5-foot-high hedge, 3 feet wide, in two to three years time. ¶ **HOW TO DO IT** ¶ For a 24-foot-long hedge, you need twelve one-year-old bare-root rosa rugosa plants and a full-sun location. Soak the roots of the roses overnight in water. For each plant dig a hole 1 foot deep and 1 foot wide, or large enough to accommodate the fanned roots. Trim and discard any bits of root that are broken or dead. Place the roots in the hole, and gradually fill the hole with a mixture of soil, sand, and well-rotted manure, leaving a slight hollow for watering. The topmost roots should be about 2 inches below the surface. ¶ Fertilize the roses just as the first new growth appears in spring, with a rose or all-purpose fertilizer. No pruning is necessary to encourage bloom, and very little to control shaping, as the growth is quite regular.

Rosa rugosa
Rosa rugosa 'Rubra', 'Alba'
3 to 5 feet tall
White, crimson

❧

What You Need
12 1-year-old bare-root plants
Sand
Well-rotted manure
Small pruning clippers
Rose or all-purpose fertilizer
24-by-4-foot area of prepared ground with full sun

❧

When to Buy
Fall and winter from mail-order catalogues and specialty nurseries

❧

When to Plant
Early spring, winter in mild-climate areas

❧

Period of Bloom
Intermittently, spring through fall

❧

Throughout my childhood, the scent of lilac conjured memories of the grandmother I knew only from turn of the century sepia photographs. According to my father, lilacs had been her favorite flower. As an adult, traveling in England and France I was captivated by the 20-foot-high hedges of purple, lavender, and white lilac that seemed to tower everywhere, overpowering passersby with their heavy fragrance that suggests slightly damp dust mingled with rosewater. ¶ Lilacs are relatively easy to grow, and they practically take care of themselves once started. ¶ To create a hedge effect with lilacs, plant as many as you want in a row, then as they grow, prune them as if they were a single unit. Depending upon your garden style, the pruning may be controlled and geometric or loose and unstructured. ¶ **HOW TO DO IT** ¶ For a 20-foot-by-6-foot hedge you need eight lilacs, 5-gallon-pot size, and a 20-by-3-foot area of prepared ground. For each plant, dig a hole 2 feet deep and 2 feet in diameter in prepared garden ground. A full-sun location is preferable except in areas with hot summers, where the lilac may need filtered shade. ¶ Fill a large bucket or sink full of water and soak the lilacs, still in their pots, to saturate the soil mix. Remove the lilacs with the soil clinging to the roots and place one in each of the prepared holes, gently fanning the roots downward and out. Gently but firmly pack garden soil around the roots, gradually filling in the holes. Water to saturate the soil. Keep the plants well watered thereafter until summer's end, when the plants will begin to go dormant. ¶ Fertilize twice a year with an all-purpose fertilizer. To prune, remove any dead growth and branches from near the base of the lilac, unless you want a very shrubby effect for your hedge.

Common Lilac
Syringa vulgaris
10 to 20 feet tall
Shades of purple and white

❦

What You Need
1- or 2-year-old lilac, 5-gallon-pot size
Small pruning clippers
Fertilizer
Lime (if soil is acid)
20-by-3-foot area of prepared ground with full sun, filtered shade in hot summer areas

❦

When to Buy
Winter through spring from nurseries

❦

When to Plant
Early spring

❦

Period of Bloom
Late spring or early summer, for three to four weeks

❦

PEONY

Peony

Paeonia lactiflora *varieties,*
especially 'Mrs. Franklin Roosevelt',
'Sarah Bernhardt'
3 feet tall
Red, pink, rose, or white

❧

What You Need
20 peony tuber clumps
Well-rotted manure, if needed
Sand, if needed
All-purpose fertilizer
20-by-1-foot area of prepared ground
with full sun, filtered shade in
hot summer areas

❧

When to Buy
August through November, from
mail-order catalogues and nurseries

❧

When to Plant
Fall

❧

Period of Bloom
Late spring or early summer, depending
upon variety, for 6 to 8 weeks

❧

Peonies are one of the classic old-fashioned flowers for fragrance. The scent ranges from delicate berry to deep nectar, depending upon variety. However, there are numerous new varieties of peonies and some of them have scant, if any, fragrance at all, so choose carefully. ¶ A hedge of peonies in full bloom is a startling garden sight. Flowers 5 to 8 inches across on foot-long stems burst forth from glistening, smooth green foliage appearing for all purposes like something Alice would have seen in Wonderland. Not only are peonies wondrous to look at, the cupped or ruffled blooms make superb, long-lasting cut flowers, and the plants themselves can be long-lived and hardy once established, although they die back in winter. Peonies must have rich, well-drained soil, but this can be created if it does not occur naturally in your garden. If needed, add a substantial amount of organic matter and sand to your soil and the decomposing organic matter will enrich it while the sand aerates it and provides drainage. Peonies must have enough winter cold to induce a dormancy period, and mild, not hot, humid weather, during the period of bloom. ¶ To create a hedge effect with peonies plant as many plants as you want in a row, keeping in mind that they die back in winter, and then trim them as if they were a single unit. ¶ **HOW TO DO IT** ¶ For a 20-foot-long hedge of peonies, you will need twenty peony tuber clumps, a sunny location, and within it a 20-by-1-foot area of prepared garden soil. Dig into the soil to a depth of 18 to 24 inches to loosen it, and work in extra organic matter before planting. For each tuber clump, dig a hole about 6 inches deep. Place the tuber clump in the hole, eyes up. If the tubers have already begun to bud, you will see tiny pinkish-red tips emerging from the ➹

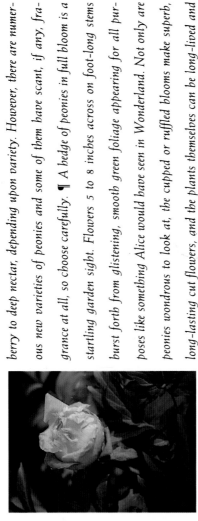

eyes. The top of the tuber clumps should be between 1 and 2 inches beneath the surface, closer to the surface in areas with light winter frosts. Cover with soil and water well to saturate. ¶ Keep peonies well-watered through spring and summer. In fall, when the plants are starting to dry and wither, cut them back to 1 inch above the surface of the ground. In early spring apply an all-purpose fertilizer.

HONEYSUCKLE

Honeysuckle
Lonicera hildebrandiana
'Giant Burmese',
L. japonica
'Halliana' (Hall's)
20 feet, 15 feet
White fading to amber, white
changing to yellow

❦

What You Need
1 plant, 1-gallon-pot size
Small pruning clippers
All-purpose fertilizer

Galvanized wire, trellis, or other support
10 square feet of prepared ground
with a full day sun, half day or
filtered sun in hot summer areas

When to Buy
Spring

❦

When to Plant
Spring

❦

Period of Bloom
Summer, until frost

❦

The garages and back-alley fences of the small southern California beach town where I grew up were covered with soft green honeysuckle vines, some of them 20 feet high and twice as wide but all of them blanketed with creamy golden-orange flowers. The flowers smelled like nectar—sweet, warm, and honeyed. We children cut pieces of the long vines to wrap around us when we played dress-up, pretending they were feather boas, or wound them into flowering tiaras. ¶ There are numerous varieties of honeysuckle, many of them fragrant. Most grow quite easily and quickly and some become rampant if not pruned back and kept under control, but their scent and the light, airy look they give to bouquets, like butterflies in flight, make it worthwhile to grow and tame the vines. ¶ To make a bower or hedge of honeysuckle, you will need to provide support for the naturally twining vines. Galvanized wire, a wooden or metal trellis, or even a clothesline pole will suffice. To prune the vines, cut them back to the woody trunk and main branches. It may be difficult emotionally to cut off the long vines, but the cuts will encourage new, luxuriant growth, which will come quickly. ¶ **HOW TO DO IT** ¶ For a 1-gallon-pot-size plant, dig a hole 18 inches wide and 18 inches deep. Meanwhile, fill a large bucket or sink full of water and soak the plant, still in its pot, until saturated. ¶ Remove the plant from the pot, gently shaking loose the mix from the roots. Examine them. If they go around and around the sides in the shape of the container, cut them back to the beginning of the circular growth. Now trim the top growth a like amount, so it is in balance with the revised root system. For example, if you ✒

have trimmed away one-third of the root growth, you should trim an equal amount of top growth. Hold the plant upright over the hole, fanning the roots out, and pack the roots with moist soil, gradually filling the hole. Place the trellis or wires approximately 10 inches away from the plant. ¶ Water the honeysuckle thoroughly and fertilize twice a year. Keep well watered throughout its growing season, removing dead vines as they appear. The following spring, fertilize again and prune.

POET'S JASMINE

Jasmine is one of the classic scents of the perfume world, being ambrosial yet light, not cloying.

Although there are numerous varieties of jasmine, it is common or poet's jasmine that is most frequently grown for fragrance and is raised commercially in southern France for the perfume industry that has been centered in Grasse since the seventeenth century. Small, white, waxy flowers dot shining, dark green foliage, and in summer, the blooming fields in the area around Grasse can scent the air for miles. ¶ Common jasmine is relatively easy to grow for the home gardener, thriving in most garden soil and having no special requirements other than a structure on which to twine and climb to create a simple bower. It needs little protection during winter, except in the harshest climates. ¶ **HOW TO DO IT** ¶ For a single vine, you need a 1-gallon-pot-size jasmine plant and a location that receives three-quarters to a full day of sun. Fill a large bucket or sink with water and soak the plant, still in its container, to saturate it. ¶ Dig a hole 18 inches deep and 18 inches wide. Gently remove the plant from the container, along with any potting mix clinging to its roots. Suspend the plant in the hole at the same planting depth it had in the container. Pack soil around the roots, gradually filling the hole. Place the trellis, wire, or other structure about 10 inches from the plant roots. Water to saturate the ground. Keep the jasmine well watered during growth and bloom. Fertilize every six weeks with a liquid fertilizer. In fall, trim the vines to maintain or direct the shape of the jasmine.

Poet's or Common Jasmine
Jasminum officinale
15 to 20 feet tall
White

❧

What You Need
1 plant, 1 gallon size
Small pruning clippers
All-purpose fertilizer
Trellis, wire, or other structure
5 square feet of prepared ground
with ¾ to a full day sun

❧

When to Buy
Spring, from nurseries and garden centers

❧

When to Plant
Spring

❧

Period of Bloom
All summer, until frost

❧

CAPTURED FRAGRANCE

For thousands of years flowers have been dried or their essence extracted by solvents or by distillation, thus extending the odor of the flower beyond its limited blooming season. An essence can in turn be added to water, soaps, and unguents, as it was historically, to further extend its uses. Hence, rosewater and oil of jasmine. ❧ To extract the essence of flowers without specialized equipment can be difficult, but it is quite easy to preserve the fragrance of flowers by drying them. Air-drying is the oldest and most classic method, but other methods include packing the material to be preserved in desiccants, such as silica gel or clean sand, oven- or, freeze-drying it, or saturating it with glycerine. ❧ In air-drying, whole flower heads, flowering stems, branches, or single petals are dried by warm, dry, circulating air, preferably out of bright sunlight that can bleach the color. Flowering stems and branches, such as roses and peonies, are best tied in loose bunches and hung upside down to dry. Whole flower heads, as of rosebuds, narcissus, and gardenias, may be spread on metal sheets to dry if they can be turned frequently; otherwise, it is better to put them on a rack or on chicken wire so that air can circulate freely. Single petals will dry readily when spread in a single layer on baking sheets. ❧ Humidity is the foe of dried flowers, and slow drying may allow mold to grow on the flowers, as will improper storage once the flowers are dried. To store, keep the dried flowers loosely packed in paper bags, boxes, or tins and keep them in a dry place where there is no danger of moisture. ❧ Once dried, the flowers can be used to make scented mixtures to distribute in bowls or baskets throughout the house, or to fill sachets to tuck into lingerie drawers or suitcases. Bundles of aromatic stems can be tied onto packages or used to scent a fire. A prearranged dried bouquet needs no further attention.

No mixture of dried flowers could be simpler or more fragrant than rose petals and lavender

What You Need

10 to 12 large rose blossoms

24 stems of lavender in bloom

8 narcissus

30 sage leaves

3 to 4 baking or other trays

Dry, warm, dark location

blossoms. However, I find that as much as I like the purity of only two flowers, I still am tempted to add a fillip to the classic potpourri. ¶ When dried, whole narcissus have the texture of light parchment, and their petals fold and twist into fine shapes that catch the tiny lavender blossoms in their edges. The creamy yellow makes a good contrast with the pink and red rose petals and the purple lavender. A few soft grey sage leaves balance the floral colors and also change the scent of the potpourri mixture ever so slightly, giving it underpinnings of camphor. ¶ Since the narcissus, roses, and lavender bloom at different times of the year, they are gathered and dried separately, then mixed together for the final composition. ¶ Some people add floral or herbal oils and a fixative when making a potpourri, but I prefer a potpourri that relies only on the scent of the flowers and leaves in the mixture. ¶ **HOW TO DO IT** ¶ For 1 pint of pot- pourri you need approximately 10 to 12 roses in bloom, 24 stems of blooming laven- der, 8 narcissus, and 30 sage leaves. Pick the flowers early in the morning before they are fully opened. Pick the herbs in the morning as well. Gently remove the petals from the roses. Leave the lavender on its stems to dry, but remove the narcissus blossoms from their stems. Discard the stems. ¶ Spread the freshly gathered rose petals, lavender flowers, narcissus blossoms, and optional sage leaves in a single layer on baking sheets or other trays. Put them in a dry, warm, dark place, such as an attic or enclosed garage. Turn them occasionally until they are dry, about several days for petals, to one week or longer for the larger blossoms. ¶ Once dry, store in paper bags or tins until ready to mix them together to make the potpourri.

SCENT STICKS

These little bundles may be made of lavender or rose stems, pieces of rosemary, or small branches of citrus—in fact of anything that has an appealing fragrance and that is woody enough to be gathered into a small bundle and tied. ¶ Scent sticks are sturdy versions of potpourri, and they can be placed in bowls around the house just as you might with rose petals. I like to use them to tie onto gift packages, and in a more extravagant gesture, to toss into the fire for the scent they give as they burn. ¶ **HOW TO DO IT** ¶ For each scent stick, gather a 2-inch-thick bundle of 5-inch-long stems, such as lavender, rose, rosemary, or citrus. If possible, the stems should include some leaves and a few flowers. Spread the stems in a single layer on baking sheets or other trays. Put them in a dry, warm, dark place, such as an attic, for a day or two to partially dry them. If gathered together into bundles while still full of moisture they are susceptible to mold. On the other hand, if they are too dry and brittle they will tend to break when you try to tie them together. ¶ Wrap each 2-inch-thick bundle with raffia or another tying material, pulling tightly enough to secure the bundle but not so tightly as to cut into the stems. Use one or two lengths per bundle. Add a separate length to use to hang the scent sticks for further drying. ¶ In a dry, warm, dark location, hang the scent sticks until thoroughly dried. Store them in paper bags or boxes until ready to use.

What You Need

Stems of lavender, rose, or rosemary, or branches of citrus, 5 inches long

1-foot lengths of burnable tying material, such as raffia or twine

Dry, warm, dark location

❧

LAVENDER SACHETS

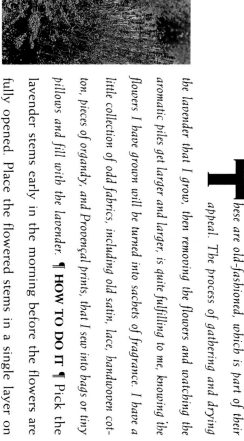

These are old-fashioned, which is part of their appeal. The process of gathering and drying the lavender that I grow, then removing the flowers and watching the aromatic piles get larger and larger, is quite fulfilling to me, knowing the flowers I have grown will be turned into sachets of fragrance. I have a little collection of odd fabrics, including old satin, lace, handwoven cotton, pieces of organdy, and Provençal prints, that I sew into bags or tiny pillows and fill with the lavender. ¶ **HOW TO DO IT** ¶ Pick the lavender stems early in the morning before the flowers are fully opened. Place the flowered stems in a single layer on baking sheets or other trays. Put them in a dry, warm, dark place, such as an attic or enclosed garage, for several days or longer, until they are fully dried. Removed the flowers from the stems. Store the flowers in paper bags or tins until ready to use. ¶ To make five sachets you need ten 4-inch-by-4-inch square pieces of fabric. To make a little bag, sew two squares together on three sides, leaving a half-inch seam. Turn the squares inside out, so that the seams are on the inside. Turn down and hem each side of the open top to make a little bag. Press flat with an iron. Fill the bag to within an inch of the top. Sew to close, leaving a half-inch seam, or tie with ribbon or lace. Repeat with the other squares.

What You Need

10 4-inch-by-4-inch squares of fabric

Needle and Thread

Lace, ribbon, or other trim (optional)

4 cups dried lavender blossoms,
about 100 stems

❦

MAIL-ORDER SOURCES FOR SPECIALTY SEEDS AND PLANTS

Some companies charge for their catalogues. Call first to check.

Antique Rose Emporium
Route 5, Box 143
Brenham, TX 77833
(409) 836-9051
A large selection of old roses.

Dutch Gardens Bulbs
P.O. Box 200
Adelphia, N.J. 07710
(908) 780-2713
(908) 780-2720 Fax
Full-page color photographs, fragrant flowers noted with banner. Wide selection.

High Country Rosarium
211 Haviland Mill Road
Brookeville, MD 20833-2311
(303) 832-4026

McClure & Zimmerman Bulbs
108 West Winnebago
P.O. Box 368
Friesland, WI 53935
(414) 326-4220
(414) 326-5769 Fax
Fine selection of fragrant tulips, narcissus, and hyacinths and many other bulbs. Illustrated with original drawings.

Mendocino Heirloom Roses
P.O. Box 670
Mendocino, CA 95470
(707) 877-1888 or (707) 937-0963
Classic rugosa and damask roses, many other unusual old roses. Lengthy descriptions; complete chart of pertinent information for all the roses in the catalogue; no illustrations.

Shepherd's Garden Seeds
Shipping Office
30 Irene Street
Torrington, CT 06970
(203) 482-3638
(203) 496-1418 Fax
or in California
(408) 335-6910
(408) 335-2080 Fax
A good selection of fragrant flowers to grow from seeds, including sweet peas. Catalogue is illustrated with original drawings.

Smith & Hawken
25 Corte Madera
Mill Valley, CA 94941
(415) 383-2000
(415) 383-7030 Fax
Selection of unusual flower seeds, many fragrant. Also bulbs, including Asiatic lilies. Illustrated with color photographs.

Thompson & Morgan
P.O. Box 1308
Jackson, NJ 08527-0308
(908) 363-2225
A vast number of seeds for perennials and annuals, including an especially good selection of sweet peas. Illustrated with color photographs.

Wayside Gardens
1 Garden Lane
Hodges, SC 29695-0001
(800) 845-1124
A number of plants, including vines, flowering shrubs, and bulbs. Illustrated with color photographs.

White Flower Farm
P.O. Box 50
Litchfield, CT 06759-0050
(203) 496-9624
A wide selection of perennials and bulbs. Beautifully illustrated catalogue.

BIBLIOGRAPHY

Ackerman, Diane.
A Natural History of the Senses.
New York: Vintage Books, 1991.

Brennan, Georgeanne, and
Luebberman, Mimi.
Beautiful Bulbs.
San Francisco: Chronicle Books, 1993.

Brennan, Georgeanne, and
Luebberman, Mimi.
Little Herb Gardens.
San Francisco: Chronicle Books, 1993.

Brooklyn Botanic Garden Record.
*Gardening for Fragrance, vol. 45, no. 3,
Handbook #121.*
Brooklyn: Brooklyn Botanic Garden,
Inc., Fall, 1989.

Green, Timothy.
"Mysterious Perfume."
Smithsonian, vol. 22, no. 3, June, 1991.

Griffiths, Trevor.
The Book of Classic Old Roses.
London: The Penguin Group, 1988.

LeGuerer, Annick.
The Mysterious and Essential Powers of Smell.
Translated by Richard Miller.
New York: Random House, 1992.

Hillier, Malcolm, and Hilton, Colin.
The Book of Dried Flowers.
New York: Simon and Schuster, 1986.

Martin, Tovah.
The Essence of Paradise.
Boston: Little, Brown and Company,
1991.

Peddie, Mary, and Lewis, Judy and John.
*Growing and Using Scented Geraniums
(Bulletin A-131).*
Pownal, Vermont: Storey/Garden Way
Publishing, 1991.

Phillips, Roger, and Rix, Martyn.
The Random House Guide to Roses.
New York: Random House, 1988.

Stuart, David, and Sutherland, James.
Plants of the Past.
London: Penguin Books, 1989.

Suskind, Patrick.
Perfume.
New York: Washington Square Press, 1986.

Vilmorin-Andrieux et Cie.
Les Fleurs de Pleine Terre.
Reprint of 1984 edition by Les Editions
1900, 1989.

Verrier, Suzanne.
Rosa Rugosa.
Deer Park: Capability's Books, 1991.

INDEX

Acknowledgments

A s with all books, it is the people involved who make them special. Our deepest thanks to them all. Bill LeBlond and Leslie Jonath, our editors at Chronicle Books, who always give their unflagging support and kindly ear; Michael Carabetta, the design director, and design coordinator Laura Lovett at Chronicle Books, and the book's designers, Bob Aufuldish and Kathy Warinner, who took our words and photos and turned them into a vision of fragrance; Carey Charlesworth, our copy editor who read the manuscript with an unswerving eye on structure; Jim Schrupp, our botanical and horticultural consultant, who scrutinized the manuscript; and thanks, as always, to The Gardener, Berkeley, California, and to Vanderbilt & Co., Florabunda, Tesora, and Hedgerow in Napa Valley, California. ¶ Many thanks, too, to The Wonderful Wags, Susan, Camilla, Marianne, Lisbeth, Sandy, Alex, Sally, Johnny, Joanne, Don and Sally, Ann, Carolee, Mimi, Sarah, Larry and Holly, Jerry, and especially to Billy and Michael for their inspiring sense of beauty. And to Bruce and Jim for their love and encouragement.